Lulu's Song

First published in 2008
by Wayland

Text copyright © Karen Wallace 2008
Illustration copyright © Lisa Williams 2008

Wayland
338 Euston Road
London NW1 3BH

Wayland Australia
Level 17/207 Kent Street
Sydney, NSW 2000

Series Editor: Louise John
Cover design: Paul Cherrill
Design: D.R.ink
Consultant: Shirley Bickler

A CIP catalogue record for this book is available from the British Library.

ISBN 9780750254021

Printed in China

Wayland is a division of Hachette Children's Books,
an Hachette Livre UK Company
www.hachettelivre.co.uk

Lulu's Song

Written by Karen Wallace
Illustrated by Lisa Williams

WAYLAND

Lulu the Parrot sat on her branch.
She listened to the sounds of
the jungle and she watched the
sun go down.

A bird whistled and a frog croaked.

She heard a cricket chirrup in the bushes and a mouse squeak on the ground.

All the different noises sounded
like music to Lulu. She closed her
eyes and went to sleep.

9

The next morning, Lulu had
a wonderful idea.

"Let's play our own music," she said
to her friends.

Everyone was very excited and
rushed off to find something
to play.

Spots the Leopard found a hollow
log that sounded like a drum.

Flora the Elephant pulled down
a bean from the top of a tree.

When she shook the bean, it made
a great rattling sound.

Monty the Monkey wanted to make
something himself.

First he found a forked branch.

Then he stretched some vines
over it.

"It's my jungle harp," he told Lulu. "It makes a great twang if I play it with my fingers."

19

Lulu couldn't find anything
to play.

She banged two nuts together with
her beak, but they broke in half.

She waved a branch but it didn't
make a noise at all.

"Don't worry," said Monty.
"You'll find something."

So Lulu kept on looking while her friends all sat and played music together.

Spots banged his drum. Flora rattled her bean and Monty made his jungle harp go twang, twang, twang.

It sounded fantastic!

"What shall I play? What shall I play?" squawked Lulu out loud.

Then she heard the sound of her own voice, and she knew just what to do.

"I shall make up my own song and sing it," cried Lulu. "Everyone loves a song!"

29

So Lulu sang a song called
'Down in the jungle,
we have fun, fun, fun!'.

And all her friends joined in, too!

START READING is a series of highly enjoyable books for beginner readers. They have been carefully graded to match the Book Bands widely used in schools. This enables readers to be sure they choose books that match their own reading ability.

The Bands are:

Pink / Band 1
Red / Band 2
Yellow / Band 3
Blue / Band 4
Green / Band 5
Orange / Band 6
Turquoise / Band 7
Purple / Band 8
Gold / Band 9

START READING books can be read independently or shared with an adult. They promote the enjoyment of reading through satisfying stories supported by fun illustrations.

Karen Wallace was brought up in a log cabin in Canada. She has written lots of different books for children, fiction and non-fiction, and even won a few awards. Karen likes writing funny books because she can laugh at her own jokes! She has two sons and two cats. The sons have grown up and left home but the cats are still around.

Lisa Williams did her first drawing at 15 months old - it was a worm! She told her mum to write 'Worm' underneath the picture. When she was five, she decided that she wanted to be an illustrator when she grew up. She has always loved drawing animals and hopes that you will enjoy this book...